AF445308

# In Green Valley, AZ, We Breed Crazy Cats To Eat Little Desert Rats. *Why?* ...

*"I told those vicious little devils I was a Hollow-eyed Killer."*
[smack, smack]

## ... because those "cute" little devils eat our car wiring like it was spaghetti!

A Paperback Series from
Go2Fun, LLC

contact@G2F.com

A Journal and Planner for those who want a place to write down appointments, names of people met, activities enjoyed and exciting stories to remember.

Green Valley Series [01] Vol. 4.01

# *Who Are You People, Anyway?*

The world has enough of the anger, hatred and *envy-besotted* babble emanating from cultural warriors, politicians and ne're-do-wells. Especially, any of those people looking at **you** right over there.

Wouldn't you agree?

So, let's have some FUN. We're all about your being amused, tickled and entertained if and when we're able to drop-kick your funny-bone into a giggle. Or, at least bring a smile to your face.

**Go2Fun Today** create and publish journals, notebooks, diaries, planners, logbooks and more. Including blank-page interiors for sketching, mind mapping or any other purpose you can imagine. All with the idea of your having FUN.

Our books make **wonderful gifts** for events, holidays, anniversary's and especially your workplace.

*Do enjoy. Smile a little. We'll all be the better for it.*

Even more Fun Stuff at www.Go2Fun.Today

*The internationally known **Talking Stick Patio** at Resort Homes, Green Valley, AZ*

Escapees from distant lands annually gather about the famous *Talking Stick Patio* of Green Valley.

Known as THE place to be for new and old friends to regale The Congregation with wonderful tales of travels, travails and raucous FUN of every sort.

And as *Ol' Fusses*, every now and then invoking empathy and sympathy with updates on all miseries known to man.

*Oh My! Such is life in Green Valley.*

# Want More?

Search Amazon Books For **"Go2Fun"**

All our **FUN STUFF** is there.

Even more Fun Stuff at www.Go2Fun.Today

# Legal Blather

OPENING ARGUMENT: *"I'm way more a ferocious Junkyard-Dog Lawyer than* **you.** *"*

CLOSING ARGUMENT: *"Like* **hell** *you are!"*



*"Why can't we all just get along?"*

Even more Fun Stuff at www.Go2Fun.Today

# Monthly Planner

Month: _________  Year: _________

| Monday | Tuesday | Wednesday | Thursday | Friday | Saturday | Sunday |
| --- | --- | --- | --- | --- | --- | --- |
| ☐ | ☐ | ☐ | ☐ | ☐ | ☐ | ☐ |
| ☐ | ☐ | ☐ | ☐ | ☐ | ☐ | ☐ |
| ☐ | ☐ | ☐ | ☐ | ☐ | ☐ | ☐ |
| ☐ | ☐ | ☐ | ☐ | ☐ | ☐ | ☐ |
| ☐ | ☐ | ☐ | ☐ | ☐ | ☐ | ☐ |

Notes:

# Monthly Planner

**Month:** _________ **Year:** _________

| Monday | Tuesday | Wednesday | Thursday | Friday | Saturday | Sunday |
|--------|---------|-----------|----------|--------|----------|--------|
|  |  |  |  |  |  |  |
|  |  |  |  |  |  |  |
|  |  |  |  |  |  |  |
|  |  |  |  |  |  |  |
|  |  |  |  |  |  |  |

**Notes:**

# Monthly Planner

Month: ________    Year: ________

| Monday | Tuesday | Wednesday | Thursday | Friday | Saturday | Sunday |
|---|---|---|---|---|---|---|
|  |  |  |  |  |  |  |
|  |  |  |  |  |  |  |
|  |  |  |  |  |  |  |
|  |  |  |  |  |  |  |
|  |  |  |  |  |  |  |

Notes:

# Monthly Planner

Month: _________ Year: _________

| Monday | Tuesday | Wednesday | Thursday | Friday | Saturday | Sunday |
| --- | --- | --- | --- | --- | --- | --- |
| | | | | | | |
| | | | | | | |
| | | | | | | |
| | | | | | | |
| | | | | | | |

Notes:

# Monthly Planner

Month: _______  Year: _______

| Monday | Tuesday | Wednesday | Thursday | Friday | Saturday | Sunday |
| --- | --- | --- | --- | --- | --- | --- |
| ☐ | ☐ | ☐ | ☐ | ☐ | ☐ | ☐ |
| ☐ | ☐ | ☐ | ☐ | ☐ | ☐ | ☐ |
| ☐ | ☐ | ☐ | ☐ | ☐ | ☐ | ☐ |
| ☐ | ☐ | ☐ | ☐ | ☐ | ☐ | ☐ |
| ☐ | ☐ | ☐ | ☐ | ☐ | ☐ | ☐ |

Notes:

# Monthly Planner

Month: _________  Year: _________

| Monday | Tuesday | Wednesday | Thursday | Friday | Saturday | Sunday |
|--------|---------|-----------|----------|--------|----------|--------|
| ☐ | ☐ | ☐ | ☐ | ☐ | ☐ | ☐ |
| ☐ | ☐ | ☐ | ☐ | ☐ | ☐ | ☐ |
| ☐ | ☐ | ☐ | ☐ | ☐ | ☐ | ☐ |
| ☐ | ☐ | ☐ | ☐ | ☐ | ☐ | ☐ |
| ☐ | ☐ | ☐ | ☐ | ☐ | ☐ | ☐ |

**Notes:**

# Monthly Planner

Month: _________ Year: _________

| Monday | Tuesday | Wednesday | Thursday | Friday | Saturday | Sunday |
|--------|---------|-----------|----------|--------|----------|--------|
| ☐ | ☐ | ☐ | ☐ | ☐ | ☐ | ☐ |
| ☐ | ☐ | ☐ | ☐ | ☐ | ☐ | ☐ |
| ☐ | ☐ | ☐ | ☐ | ☐ | ☐ | ☐ |
| ☐ | ☐ | ☐ | ☐ | ☐ | ☐ | ☐ |
| ☐ | ☐ | ☐ | ☐ | ☐ | ☐ | ☐ |

Notes:

# Monthly Planner

Month: _______ Year: _______

| Monday | Tuesday | Wednesday | Thursday | Friday | Saturday | Sunday |
|--------|---------|-----------|----------|--------|----------|--------|
| ☐ | ☐ | ☐ | ☐ | ☐ | ☐ | ☐ |
| ☐ | ☐ | ☐ | ☐ | ☐ | ☐ | ☐ |
| ☐ | ☐ | ☐ | ☐ | ☐ | ☐ | ☐ |
| ☐ | ☐ | ☐ | ☐ | ☐ | ☐ | ☐ |
| ☐ | ☐ | ☐ | ☐ | ☐ | ☐ | ☐ |

Notes:

# Monthly Planner

Month: _______ Year: _______

| Monday | Tuesday | Wednesday | Thursday | Friday | Saturday | Sunday |
|---|---|---|---|---|---|---|
|  |  |  |  |  |  |  |
|  |  |  |  |  |  |  |
|  |  |  |  |  |  |  |
|  |  |  |  |  |  |  |
|  |  |  |  |  |  |  |

Notes:

# Monthly Planner

Month: _________ Year: _________

| Monday | Tuesday | Wednesday | Thursday | Friday | Saturday | Sunday |
|---|---|---|---|---|---|---|
| ☐ | ☐ | ☐ | ☐ | ☐ | ☐ | ☐ |
| ☐ | ☐ | ☐ | ☐ | ☐ | ☐ | ☐ |
| ☐ | ☐ | ☐ | ☐ | ☐ | ☐ | ☐ |
| ☐ | ☐ | ☐ | ☐ | ☐ | ☐ | ☐ |
| ☐ | ☐ | ☐ | ☐ | ☐ | ☐ | ☐ |

**Notes:**

# Monthly Planner

Month: _________ Year: _________

| Monday | Tuesday | Wednesday | Thursday | Friday | Saturday | Sunday |
|--------|---------|-----------|----------|--------|----------|--------|
| ☐ | ☐ | ☐ | ☐ | ☐ | ☐ | ☐ |
| ☐ | ☐ | ☐ | ☐ | ☐ | ☐ | ☐ |
| ☐ | ☐ | ☐ | ☐ | ☐ | ☐ | ☐ |
| ☐ | ☐ | ☐ | ☐ | ☐ | ☐ | ☐ |
| ☐ | ☐ | ☐ | ☐ | ☐ | ☐ | ☐ |

Notes:

# Monthly Planner

Month: _________ Year: _________

| Monday | Tuesday | Wednesday | Thursday | Friday | Saturday | Sunday |
|--------|---------|-----------|----------|--------|----------|--------|
| ☐ | ☐ | ☐ | ☐ | ☐ | ☐ | ☐ |
| ☐ | ☐ | ☐ | ☐ | ☐ | ☐ | ☐ |
| ☐ | ☐ | ☐ | ☐ | ☐ | ☐ | ☐ |
| ☐ | ☐ | ☐ | ☐ | ☐ | ☐ | ☐ |
| ☐ | ☐ | ☐ | ☐ | ☐ | ☐ | ☐ |

Notes:

# Talking Stick Patio

*They're going to say **WHAT** in the Talking Stick Patio?*

Even more FUN Stuff at www.Go2Fun.Today

Full-timers —like we *Ol' Fusses*— in Green Valley, AZ patiently wait out the summer's Big Heat. All the while looking forward <mostly> for the arrival of SnowBirds, RainBirds and StrangeBirds for the winter season.

We say "mostly" because every year, a few WildAssBirds invade the shopping center parking lots with fried-egg eyes fully blinded to reality.

<u>Dateline Green Valley</u>:

Delighted to have survived *The Battle Of Safeway Parking Lot,* war weary veterans fly home — *thanking GAWD —* they've lived through the first mission. And thinking how much safer their street was wherever they came from.

[FYI: During the height of battle, snarky word-salads of *"Hot Damn!", "Oooooooohhh Sheet!"* and *"Mercy, Jesus!"* dive-bombed their ears from every quarter. They lived.]

Even more FUN Stuff at <u>www.Go2Fun.Today</u>

Anyway, we Full-timers truly welcome our Winter Nomads every year and can't wait to hear their tales, travails and torments of the year gone by. Their stories about life.

Homing in from every compass point, they find their Green Valley winter nests with the ease of Monarch butterflies.

Golfers fervently flail the courses, bicyclists pedal the metal and Pickle Ball players tickle their fancy at every opportunity. Never mind the "robust" swimmers whaling away pretending they're preparing for a Triathlon.

*How long will it last?* Well, some have returned to Talking Stick Patio every year for 20 years! And we think they'll continue as long as their health allows.

*Such is life in Green Valley, AZ.*

Even more FUN Stuff at <u>www.Go2Fun.Today</u>

# Story Tellers All

**DrumTalker**, the mascot of Talking Stick Patio

Talking Stick Patio in the Resort Homes neighborhood of Green Valley is an unusual place to experience.

We *Ol' Fusses* at Go2Fun Today are well-traveled beyond the county line. However, nowhere on earth we've been matches the pleasant *gemütlichkeit* [loose translation — cozy atmosphere] we've enjoyed here.

It's a wonderfully fertile farm for stories of all kinds. Over the coming years we plan to include some of these stories in many of our journals, diaries, notebooks and planners.

We invite you to saunter with us awhile as you record your own activities, memories and stories in one of our books.

Most cordially,
Glenn & Dee Dee Flock,
Talking Stick Talkers, a.k.a *Ol' Fusses*

# Want More?

Search Amazon Books for **"*Go2Fun*"**

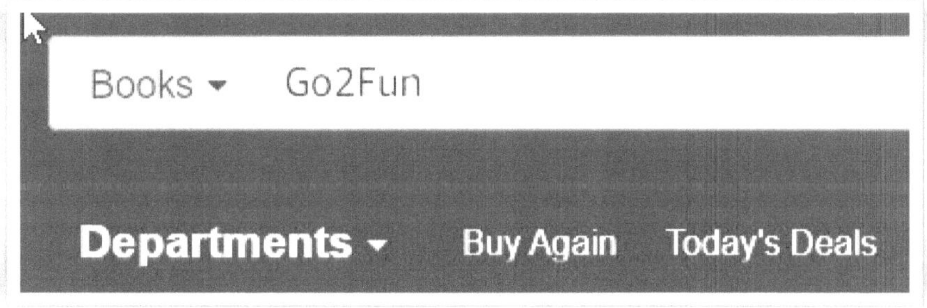


All our FUN STUFF is there.

Even more FUN Stuff at www.Go2Fun.Today